The FOX and the FEATHER

Written and Illustrated by
KENDALL LANNING, BA, CCLS

OMAHA, NEBRASKA

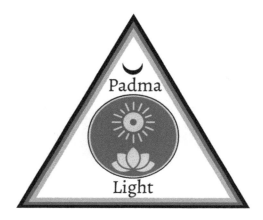

Contact the publisher by visiting www.padmalight.com

Hardcover: 978-1-7353151-1-9
Paperback: 978-1-7353151-2-6
Mobi: 978-1-7353151-3-3
EPUB: 978-1-7353151-4-0
Library of Congress Cataloging Number: 2020911830

Cataloging in Publication data on file with the publisher.
Publishing coordination by Concierge Marketing Inc.

Printed in the United States of America
10 9 8 7 6 5 4 3 2 1

Thank You...

To my mother, Judy. She has always been my biggest supporter and role model. She inspires me to never give up, and encourages me to live out all my dreams with passion and integrity. Growing up, she nurtured my uniqueness, validated my feelings, and honored my truth. With deep gratitude I am using this message as a way to humbly honor her strength, compassion, and motherly love.

To Tami Hoffman, my spiritual guru, amazing friend, and mystic. She continues to hold space for me to peel back the layers of my soul so that my authentic self can shine through. She gave me the gift of letting go of fear, trusting, listening, and opening up my heart to love.

MJ Rounds, who always showed up, unconditionally loving everyone and everything. Her love for dogs inspired me to assure the book gets into animal clinics to inspire families who are grieving the loss a pet.

The Fox and the Cardinal were
the best of friends.

They even slept together
on the coldest of nights.

One day the Cardinal could not play. He explained
to the Fox that he was very sick and dying.

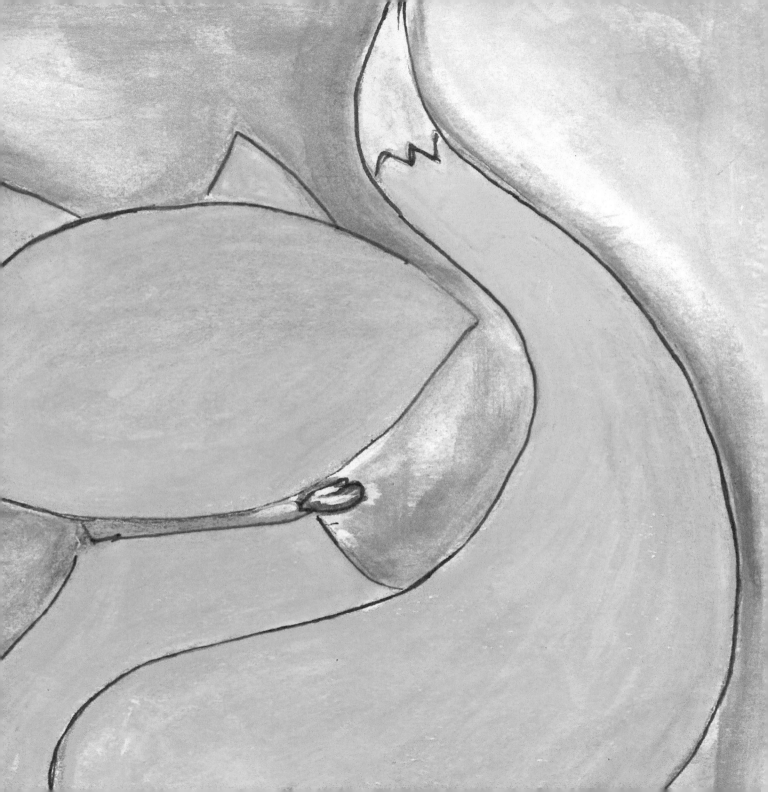

The Fox began to cry,
"Why? I do not understand."

Cardinal responded, "We cannot
always understand things, but please
remember I will be with you forever,
and will come to you in signs."

"One of those signs will be a feather and you will know that I am near."

So that night the Fox
covered the Cardinal
with his favorite scarf
and said, "Good night."

The next morning at sunrise he waved goodbye to his best friend.

The Fox missed his friend every day.
When he needed him the most, he would
always find a feather.

And he knew that the Cardinal was flying
above him, although he could not see him.

Other signs spirit can let you know they are near:

Dreams, Music, Coins, Lights, Scents, Clouds

What are some ways that your loved one may show they are near?

Activity

Get a piece of paper and write down or draw some special memories or times your loved one may let you know they are near.

For more resources, tools, and activities, go to

www.PadmaLight.com

Everyone grieves differently. Children also perceive death differently depending on their developmental stage and their concepts of death. It is important to tune into the individual needs of each child, providing a safe and supportive space for them to express their feelings. Be honest with children and use concrete language and developmentally appropriate language. What is not told to them gives them room to make up their own stories about the situations regarding death. The healing process for grief is ongoing and unpredictable. When grieving and/or holding space for someone that is grieving, it is important to remember self-care to assist in nourishing your heart.

Be prepared to answer questions and be TRUTHFUL AND HONEST

- Give children choices

- Validate feelings and encourage putting emotions into words

- Engage in memory making and memory discussions

- Remain available

- Allow children to play, talk and recreate

- Maintain routine as much as possible

- Reach out to local support groups

- Seek professional help

- Use concrete words such as "death or died" instead of "pass away"

Ages 0-2

- Increase Crying
- Irritability
- Clingy
- Change in Eating Patterns

Ages 2-4

- Think Death is Reversible or Not Permanent
- Crying/Irritability
- Temper Tantrums
- Disturbances in Sleep/Bedwetting
- Behavior Regressions-Example: May have been toilet trained and suddenly having accidents
- Fears of Abandonment
- Repetitive Questions about Death: Why's? How's?

Ages 4-7

- Physical Complaints
- Behavior Regressions
- Repetitive Questions
- Disturbances in Sleep/Bedwetting/Nightmare
- Quick to Change Emotions: Example: One minute grieving and the next playing
- Feel Responsible for the Death
- Fears of Abandonment
- Thoughts of Guilt

Ages 7-11

- Acting Out
- Experiences Guilt
- Difficulty Concentrating
- Exhibit Aggressive or Impulsive Behavior
- Expresses Wide Range of Emotions
- Asking Detailed Questions about Death
- Withdrawal
- School Difficulties

Ages 11-18

- Confusion of Identity Role within Family
- Thoughts of Self-Harm
- Engage in Risky or Dangerous Behavior
- Sleep Disturbances and Exhaustion
- Hyper-vigilance
- Abuse Substances such as Alcohol and Drugs
- Withdrawal
- School Difficulties

Kendall Lanning is a Certified Child Life Specialist
and Certified Yoga Instructor. She works closely with
pediatric patients and their families helping them cope with
hospitalizations, illness, trauma, loss and bereavement. She
finds her creative outlet through painting and was intuitively
guided to write and illustrate a children's book that will
help children cope with death and grief.

Through her personal yoga journey she found a deep connection
to her spiritual path, allowing the space for self-care, healing
and intention setting. She finds reassurance and comfort when
she listens to the signs and messages from her angels and is
hoping to share the gift through this book. The intention of
this book is to enhance conversations of remembrance, in the
hopes to give peace to the grieving heart in knowing that
their loved one is still with them.

CPSIA information can be obtained
at www.ICGtesting.com
Printed in the USA
BVHW022321030921
615690BV00030B/760